THE BEAUTY IN REBUILDING

THE BEAUTY IN REBUILDING
THERE IS LIFE AFTER P.A.I.N.

JESSICA STEPHENSON

PALMETTO
P U B L I S H I N G
Charleston, SC
www.PalmettoPublishing.com

© 2024 Jessica Stephenson
All rights reserved.
No portion of this book may be reproduced,
stored in a retrieval system, or transmitted in
any form by any means–electronic, mechanical,
photocopy, recording, or other–except for
brief quotations in printed reviews,
without prior permission of the author.

Hardcover ISBN: 9798822954137
Paperback ISBN: 9798822954144
eBook ISBN: 9798822954151

All scripture references in the book
are from the *New King James Version.*

When you are beautifully broken by God,
discovering the true beauty in your
rebuilding process becomes easy.
– Jessica Stephenson

ACKNOWLEDGEMENTS

I am extremely grateful to everyone who has been instrumental in my life's journey, who assisted and encouraged me to step outside of my comfort zones, to do the work, and to embrace healing. I am thankful for my parents, Mr. and Mrs. Jerry D. Randle, for modeling the Christian lifestyle, your unconditional love, and never giving up on me. To my amazing son, Chandler D. Nobles, I am blessed that God allowed me to be your mother. You changed my life for the better, you are my heartbeat and my love for you is endless. To my sisters in Christ, Shawonna Metcalf and Joyce Wilkerson, thank you for always believing in me, especially when I doubted myself. A special thanks to my counselor, Honour R. Sithole, for your guidance, keeping me accountable, and believing in me that I could experience true healing. Finally, thank you to my friend and future, Christopher Shaver for your love and support.

TABLE OF CONTENTS

Foreword: My Mother's Testimony xi

Introduction 1

Chapter 1: Stolen Innocence 7

Chapter 2: Suffering in Silence 19

Chapter 3: Settling for Less 33

Chapter 4: The Breaking 40

Chapter 5: The Stages of Healing 50

Chapter 6: The Evolution of You 59

Chapter 7: Conclusion 71

Resources 75

References 77

FOREWORD: MY MOTHER'S TESTIMONY

One midmorning, after welcoming our new baby girl into the world, it was a few weeks after Jerry and I brought Jessica home from the hospital. It was a normal day, and I had just put her in her crib for a nap; a short time later the excitement of having a newborn in our lives again made me eager to hold her. So I picked her up, carried her in the living room and sat in my rocker to change her diaper. I soon noticed that she seemed to be having difficulties with breathing. Suddenly she stopped breathing altogether, and that is when I started to panic.

I called 911, and an ambulance arrived quickly; everything happened so fast. The EMT workers rushed in and immediately began trying to get Jessica breathing again, but their attempts were unsuccessful. We were all rushing out of the house into the ambulance and heading for the hospital. I watched as the EMT workers continued to work on my baby girl. All I could think was, "Lord, please don't take my child away; you just gave her to me." I began to pray fearlessly that God would work a miracle. A few family members and close friends arrived in the ER, and we prayerfully waited together.

After some time the attending ER physician came to tell us that she was breathing fine now but also said that he couldn't give us a definitive answer as to why she stopped breathing. But God! We all lifted praises to God. The doctors released her, and we went home that afternoon. Looking back, I believe God led me to get her out of her crib at the time that I did; otherwise, I truly believe that it would have been a tragic outcome. Jessica has a calling over her life, and the devil tried to destroy the plans of God even before her life really began, and I know this to be true; I stand firmly on the scriptures below. What started out as a terrifying experience that morning, God immediately turned around before the end of day. I knew that Jessica was going to do amazing things in her life; she is very special to me, I love her dearly, and I am so grateful that God protected my baby girl.

Psalm 118:17*: I shall not die, but live, and declare the works of the Lord.*
Philippians 1:6*: Being confident of this very thing, that He who has begun a good work in you will complete it until the day of Jesus Christ.*

A Mother's Love and Testimony,
Zellean "Becky" Randle

INTRODUCTION

When you think about the word *rebuilding* what comes to mind? You may think that a loss has occurred somewhere or at some point, because there wouldn't be a need to rebuild, right?

The rebuilding process doesn't always look pretty nor is it easy, and it can be extremely time-consuming. Often it gets messy before you are able to see the beauty that lies deeply within. So I decided to look up the definition of *rebuilding*. The *Webster's Dictionary* says, "Rebuilding means to build something again that has been damaged or destroyed." It can also mean to repair, replace, restrengthen, or reinforce something. Additionally, rebuilding can involve making extensive structural repairs or remodeling and restoring something to a former better state.

The Bible says in **_Genesis 1:27:_** _So, God created man in His own image; in the image of God, He created Him: male and female He created them._ God's word tells us that we were created to be like Him, blameless, pure, and whole, but not broken. **_Genesis 1:31_** says, _Then God saw everything that He had made, and indeed it was very good._

We must never forget that Satan is real, and he has a different agenda from God. He hates God and everything God is, which is you and me. Throughout my life and being constantly attacked by the enemy, I discovered that his only purpose is to destroy everything God created. In this book I will share some of my personal moments, along with intimate conversations I've experienced with God, as He revealed my life purpose through various revelations and visions and while spending quiet time with Him. Transparency has not always been an easy thing for me to do, I admit, and it's okay; I'm human. This is something that I struggled with, but God has given me a testimony, and He spared my life. I live for a reason, a purpose, and His vision to fulfill my calling in this life. I have learned through my life journey that without a deep level of vulnerability partnered with being authentic, true healing cannot be manifested.

The purpose of this book is to encourage you that no matter what your past looks like, what you have done, or the adversities you are currently facing, God will restore your life.

The Bible says in **Matthew 19:26**: *With men this is impossible, but with God all things are possible.*

Jeremiah 29:11: *For I know the thoughts that I think toward you, says the Lord, thoughts of peace and not of evil, to give you a future and a hope.*

If you are still breathing, then God has a plan for your life. Throughout this book I am going to challenge you to develop a deep relationship with God, withholding nothing as He guides you through this thing called "life." Not just going to church every Sunday and Bible study on the weekdays, but instead spending time in His word by removing all distractions and allowing the heavenly Father to speak directly to you. The Scripture is true; we can't do anything without God. However, there is a caveat to this: first you must be willing to be vulnerable and transparent with YOURSELF and with Abba, our Father, to fully experience transformation. Being self-aware and acknowledging that change is needed in your life is an imperative part in the healing process. God is in full control of everything that has and will take place in your life, and He will make a way when you think there is no way. God wants to do a NEW thing in you. A new journey, new chapter, new beginnings—I believe that the new you is ready to come forth.

So? Are YOU ready to finally embrace the life God always intended for you to have?

The Bible says in ***Ephesians 2:13****: But now in Christ Jesus you who once were far off have been brought near by the blood of Christ.*

The Scripture tells us that you are never too far from the love of God. Regardless of if you are a believer in Christ or non-believer; He loves you dearly, no matter where you are or what you've done. It is God's desire to have a deep relationship with you. Are you ready to break free from the pain, the hurt, the disappointments, the self-doubt, the failures, the fears, the insecurities, the toxic behaviors, the anxiety, and most importantly living with many regrets? Why continue to settle for an autopilot version of yourself when God desires for you to experience an abundant life and so do I?

The Bible says in **Isaiah 43:19**: *Behold, I will do a new thing; now it shall spring forth; shall ye not know it? I will even make a way in the wilderness, and rivers in the desert.*

Lessons from God are presented in two ways: by His teachings through the word of God and by life experiences. I understand that God allows us to go through situations both good and bad to help develop us into what He has called us to do. Despite the hardships and adversities the world throws at us daily, God declares His promises through His word.

The Bible says in **Hebrews 13:5**: *I will never leave you nor forsake you.*

My past has not been perfect, but I will walk with you each step of the way and show you how God gave me beauty for my ashes. I was graciously blessed with a reset and a blank canvas. God restored my entire life, but this time the final picture looks completely different from the original.

I pray that you are inspired through my testimony. To God be the glory, because there is life after P.A.I.N. as you discover the beauty in your rebuilding.

Beautifully Broken,

Jessica Stephenson

CHAPTER 1: STOLEN INNOCENCE

I was born and raised on the east side of Fort Worth, Texas known as Meadowbrook and I am the baby girl to Jerry and Becky Randle. I have an older sister named Tiffany; we are four years and three months apart. Just like any sisters, we had a love-hate relationship while growing up. Meaning that on some days we were the best of friends, but on our off days, it was pure hell. If you have siblings, I'm sure you can relate. I was blessed to be raised in a two-parent household, and my parents worked very hard to make sure that my sister and I lived well by having the necessities of life.

Most importantly, our household was built on faith in God. I was saved and became a believer in Christ Jesus at a very young age. My parents were active within my uncle's church called, Faith Sanctuary Christ Holy Sanctified Church, where we attended all my childhood. My dad was the director of the Sunday school (which he absolutely loved), played bass guitar, and also preached. My mother was the director of music, choir lead, and preached the word of God. My sister and I sang together, and we were known as "The Randle Girls." Man! We use to sing all over the city of Fort Worth and Dallas at various churches, family reunions, and even funerals. We truly had a gift, and God graced us with His anointing every time we were blessed with a stage to sing on. Even though life looked good from the outside looking in, I personally was dealing with many demons.

I was born and raised in the 1980s, and trusting people in the neighborhood was the norm, unlike today. I was the type of kid who loved to be outside and hanging with friends. Being outside felt like I had broken free from a cage that no longer served me any purpose, like a butterfly breaking free from its cocoon, which I will explain in detail in a later chapter. I lived three houses down from my best friend named Kimberly, and we were inseparable. I watched out for Kim as if she was my own sister but born from another mother. We attended the same elementary and middle school until her parents moved away before starting our high school years, which totally broke my heart. She didn't have any sisters, only one brother named John.

Kim and I had a very close bond since I was never close to my own sister due to our age difference while growing up. I resonated with Kim; we were very similar in many ways; for example, settling for not being one of the popular kids at school or having the desire to be, being bullied, and being talked about. We viewed life as if we didn't have a care in the world, and we created a space to write our own stories that looked different from everyone else's. Fitting in and being a follower was not our focus; we just wanted to explore living life freely from the parameters of walking in the shadows of others. When I saw Kim, I didn't see color or religion as areas to be judgmental about. I only saw my best friend, someone who I loved dearly and cared for.

We currently live in a world that casts judgment first and thinks later, an extremely dangerous position to lead from. I truly believe that this is a prime example of how so many of our children are caught up in social media, being judged, and being hateful and cruel to one another, often trying to be like others, meanwhile neglecting their true, authentic selves and creativity. What if we all made a conscious decision of accepting ourselves just as God created us and loving everything about it? Truly falling in love with yourself. Self-love is the foundation that allows us to be assertive, set healthy boundaries, and feel proud of who we are. I believe that by adopting this one important behavior, we would start to live in a much better world than we do today.

One hot Saturday evening in the year of 1990, at the age of six years old, it was a normal day of riding my bike outside, while my dad worked on his 1972 El Camino in our home garage. That day I was riding solo because my bestie (Kim) was out of town with her family. Where I grew up, the neighbors in the community watched out for one another and acted with kindness. A trusted neighbor that my family knew very well and was well-known in the neighborhood invited me into his home to have a Popsicle. Popsicles were my favorite! This was nothing out of the ordinary, because my friends and I often received Popsicles and other goodies from this neighbor all the time; so without hesitation, I decided to enter his home. But that day was different.

Before I could realize what was happening, I was sexually violated. It happened so fast that I was unable to assess the dangers of entering his home by myself. There was no exchange of words just actions. I never for once suspected that he would be bold enough to do such an act while my father was literally down the street. This was somewhere I thought was a safe place, but I was completely wrong, and I was just a child. I was told to never say a word because it would be our "little secret." I was promised an unlimited supply of Popsicles, candy, and whatever else I wanted, but the only caveat was to never tell anyone what happened that day.

My entire life changed, and something deeply inside me broke, but I didn't quite understand what it was. A piece of me was stolen that I thought I would never get back. In the culture that I grew up in, children were seen and not heard. I was afraid to speak up about what took place that day, and I was left with so much pain and confusion. All I wanted to do was crawl under my bed and cry my eyes out. It was the beginning of the devil's seed of destruction planted deeply into my life.

From that point on, I was never the same. I was ashamed, hurt, and disappointed in myself, because I believed that it was all my fault for being so stupid to enter a home that I was never supposed to be in. I thought to myself that if my parents knew what I had done, I would be in more trouble. Although the actual abuse only took a few minutes, which felt like a lifetime, the traumatic effects of it lasted for many years. Due to the shame I felt, I promised to never tell a soul. I lived with this abuse without saying a word until I was an adult before I was brave enough to talk about it. Although I finally gained the courage to speak up, I was still broken inside due to its effects, while self-sabotaging myself and believing that my road to healing would almost be impossible. Life growing up looked very different for me, never really knowing or even attempting to embrace my worth growing into adulthood. I held onto the shame and guilt for many years. My innocence was stolen from me. It was the beginning of my brokenness, which would ultimately change the trajectory, the decisions, and choices that I made in my life.

Have you ever been a victim of someone else's neglect, abuse, or mistreatment? Or have you been hurt by someone in the church, a close friend, or family member? Well, I can relate to you, and I know exactly how you feel. Often we like to paint a picture or a facade of being this perfect person or living a stainless life, but deep down we are hurting inside, and it's okay. Do you remember when I mentioned early on how I'm going to challenge you to open your eyes and heart to start seeing the real you? The gateway to the soul is through the eyes. You owe it to yourself to be transparent in this moment. Something in your life has caused you to experience brokenness on some level or even made you feel rejected. So I am challenging you to write letters to who hurt you, explain how it made you feel, how it changed you, and the short- and long-term effects of their actions.

The purpose of this challenge is to have you release every feeling and emotion associated. This challenge is not to be rushed through, but instead take your time. Think about it…If you had the opportunity to really express yourself and not be forced to suppress it all, what would that truly look like for you? I bet you would feel so free and less weighed down, right? Upon completing your letters and reading this book, I challenge you to literally burn each of them—yes burn! And please exercise safety. This task may not make sense to you right now, but trust me—it will later. It's something about seeing those actual letters catch on fire and disintegrate in front of you. The letters represent all the things you wanted and needed to say, including the emotions. And the fire represents closure or the ending of a season never to be recreated again.

Let's take a moment to really dissect this, because true healing is not a sprint but a marathon. I'm sure you are wondering why I am challenging you in this way, and it's simple; before you can tap into true and authentic healing, you must first be honest and vulnerable with yourself, and it's okay not to be okay. Realizing where you are mentally and emotionally is important. Being authentic means coming from a real place from within, the core of you. When you can step into acknowledging what really hurts you and submitting all the pain to God, the devil starts to lose his power over your mind, over what hurt you, the rejection, and the abuse. When you finally arrive at this point, the devil has absolutely no choice but to flee.

The Bible says in ***James 4:7****: Therefore, submit to God, resist the devil and he will flee from you.*

2 Timothy 1:7*: For God has not given us a spirit of fear, but of power and of love and of a sound mind.*

Isaiah 26:3*: You will keep him in perfect peace, whose mind is stayed on You, because he trusts in You.*

These scriptures explain how we (God's children) are protected from the evil one by submitting our brokenness to God, and He will keep our minds in perfect peace. Yes, we live in a fallen, sinful world, and therefore, we cannot escape experiencing tests and trials, but we were redeemed by the blood of Jesus when He sacrificed Himself on the cross for you and me. Our debts, our sins, and our failures were all paid in full by the shedding of His blood.

The Bible says in ***1 Corinthians 15:3****: For I delivered to you first of all that which I also received: that Christ died for our sins according to the Scriptures.*

God will never leave you nor forsake you; when you fully believe in His promises through His word, you will begin to see your pain, the things that hurt you and all the disappointments in a different way. Although we live in a broken world, the Bible says the just and the unjust will be tested. God allows us to go through difficulties for many reasons. To help build our faith, to experience the hand of God in our lives, and to bless us with a testimony to share with others by giving them encouragement as we direct all back to Christ. I have learned through my personal life that when God wants to bring elevation or send a blessing down from heaven, it is often wrapped in a difficulty. But remember that God is with you every step of the way, and He has the final say in everything, both good and bad, that you will face in this life.

The Bible says in **Psalm 31:4**: *Pull me out of the net which they have secretly laid for me, for You are my strength.*

John 10:10: *The thief (the devil) does not come except to steal, and to kill, and to destroy. I have come that they may have life, and that they may have it more abundantly.*

These scriptures tell us that the devil's only assignment is to destroy you, plain and simple. This doesn't mean that you settle for living in fear but instead live above your carnal mindset, knowing that we don't wrestle against flesh and blood. The real battle is being fought in the spiritual realm. The spiritual realm is a world or realm inhabited by spirits, both good and evil, of various spiritual manifestations. It is also the realm of energy that permeates the universe and where God dwells.

The Bible says in **Ephesians 6:10–13**: *Finally, my brethren, be strong in the Lord and in the power of His might. Put on the whole armor of God that you may be able to stand against the wiles of the devil. For we do not wrestle against flesh and blood, but against principalities, against powers, against the rulers of the darkness of this age, against spiritual hosts of wickedness in the heavenly places. Therefore take up the whole armor of God that you may be able to withstand in the evil day, and having done all, to stand.*

These scriptures tell us that we need to look beyond what our eyes can see in the flesh and how we feel in the natural, to guard ourselves by putting on the whole armor of God. What our eyes see is temporary. God has already equipped us with His word, and it is the only tool we can use to fight against the devil's attacks.

CHAPTER 2: SUFFERING IN SILENCE

Eleven years later, it was the year 2001; I was seventeen years old, and I had learned to suppress the sexual abuse and the emotions. I lived my life on an autopilot version of myself. Being forced to smile even when I wanted to cry and responding with, "I'm good" whenever others asked how I was doing. I was so numb to the pain; I wasn't being true to myself; expressing my feelings was something that I didn't honestly know how to do. I was afraid of being judged by others and being blamed for my stupidity all those years ago and regretting the decision that had put me in a position to be abused. And for that I vowed to myself to never say a word; I couldn't imagine bearing the weight of more pain, or disappointment, because the guilt was already unbearable.

Early one Sunday morning, I awoke to a beautiful day; my Sunday outfit and shoes were already picked out. I was filled with excitement, ready for the Sunday school lesson, but I quickly realized that my dad wasn't getting dressed but instead pacing the living room floor with a serious look on his face. Then my mother comes out the bedroom, heading to the living room to meet my dad. "Girls! Your mother and I need to talk to you. Come here, please!" said my dad.

My sister and I met my parents and sat down together with strange looks upon our faces; we didn't know what to think, but our hearts were beating fast as we looked at one another from the corners of our eyes. I was thinking to myself: is the world ending, or did someone die? I didn't know what to think. My dad started with, "I know this is going to be tough to receive, but your mom and I have been called into pastoral ministry, and we both have accepted the call from God." God began speaking to their hearts several months before, and they knew deep down that it was God calling them out to be a shepherd, and God would bring the people He wanted them to lead.

At first I didn't know how to respond to such news. Was I supposed to be happy or angry? I was in a state of confusion, a place that I knew all too well, stemming from my past. "So what does this exactly mean? What happens now? If we don't leave soon, we will be late for Sunday school," I said in my response to my parents. Not fully accepting what they had just said. My dad began to tell us that, going forward, we would no longer be members of my uncle's church, and we were called to start our own ministry inside the home until God instructed us that it was time to move. Restoration Ministries was birthed that very day. I wasn't thrilled at all about the news; all I wanted to do was go to church and be surrounded by my family and friends, a place that I had found comfort in. But instead I was about to be stripped away from the church that I had literally grew up in, and I would no longer be a part of the community that I was so familiar with.

Most people view the church as a place of refuge, a place to find healing, peace, and salvation, but for me the church became my safe place, better yet my comfort zone. I was able to hide my pain and rejection very well; no one knew exactly what I was secretly battling with from within. Can you relate?

We all have something that we consider a comfort zone whether it's a place, a person, or a possession. A comfort zone is described as a place or situation where one feels safe or at ease and without stress. Although a comfort zone can be known as a form of security, it can also become a place of complacency and stagnation, and we all know that nothing good comes from being complacent. Growth cannot inhabit a comfort zone.

While settling within my comfort zone, I was able to fit in and hide behind a mask of deeply rooted pain and guilt that I'd suppressed for over eleven years. I personally didn't like the idea of walking away from the church I had grew up in. Too many memories, both good and bad, and I was left completely devasted, the same exact feeling when my bestie moved away from our neighborhood. My parents expected my sister and I to step up to help build our new ministry. It was a very stressful and challenging transition for my entire family. As a young teenager, I didn't understand the major impacts the new calling on my parents' life would have on me. Becoming a preacher's kid was not on my "to do" list at all. I had so many thoughts and mixed emotions that were extremely hard to process or even find the words to express how I felt. I was battling with my own personal issues that I'd never told anyone about—the sexual abuse that had occurred in my past—I was still being haunted by its negative effects. So I decided to suppress my feelings once again by becoming numb to it all. At that point in my life, it became second nature, and I was literally a pro at it.

As I reflect on how I felt, I struggled with the ability to welcome or even experience change by refusing to make a conscious decision to step outside of my comfort zone, regardless of the exposure it would bring upon my life. Even though I settled to live a life within the parameters of my self-made comfort zone, it was full of darkness and unrest, and I was constantly lying to myself that I was okay. I desperately wanted to break free from the bondage and the agony. But I didn't quite know how to even start, and that is when I started hearing the voice of the devil. It is something that I cannot put into words, and it gives me chills right now as I even think about it.

The voice was extremely conniving, sneaky, and calculated. I knew religion and church very well, but I didn't have a real relationship with God.

Which is two totally different things. I knew how to conduct myself while in church; I also knew all the right words to say, yet I was struggling deeply. I was being attacked by the devil, and his plans were to destroy me. I began to believe his lies that I wasn't good enough, that I didn't deserve better, I would forever live in a state of bondage, and that it was all my fault; no one was going to believe or love me anymore. And now being forced to step into the shoes of being a preacher's kid was another form of unnecessary self-afflicted pressure I opened the door too. Becoming a "PK," it seemed like all eyes were on me, and the news spread like wildfire. Being faced with the many stereotypes of what others believed how a preacher's kid should act was horrendous. It felt like I was living in the shadows of a title that I could never live up to, especially due to my own brokenness. I was a teenager trying to discover who I was while fighting my own demons. I was born and raised in the church, I believed in God, but I had never experienced God in an intimate or personal way for myself. Some of the constant stereotypes I heard from strangers and individuals that I knew were:

- A PK is a freak, a wild child; she thinks she's better than us, a future preacher in the making.
- PKs are the worst, being too privileged.
- And the list goes on and on.

Most people don't understand the damage they can cause when making assumptions about pastors' children and not knowing the pressures they may already be facing. Some people feel that preachers' kids are expected to act and live a holy lifestyle and maintain their purity by avoiding worldly mistakes. We must remember that we are all humans, created by God in His image, but wrapped in sinful flesh, which means no one is perfect. I was faced with so much pressure in my life that led me down a path of mental depression. But one thing I need to highlight: let's not negate the call to pastoral ministry my parents received from God. My parents were pastors for over twenty years, until God called my dad home in November of 2021. My mom now continues with the vision and call for the church.

As time progressed I fell into a deeper state of mental depression and anxiety, still not fully understanding the medical ramifications. First my innocence was stolen at a young age, I was bullied in middle school, and now I was feeling the pressures of fulfilling a role of "perfection" being a preacher's kid. My mind was fighting against me in a war that was created in my own head, with no escape in sight. I was in a constant battle of finding my identity, while suffering in silence. Seeking for someone or something to help validate who I was in my world of chaos. Identity is shaped by life experiences and social and cultural factors, and it serves multiple functions that provides meaning, direction, and a sense of self-control.

What is the importance of someone knowing their identity? A person's identity emerges during childhood as children start to comprehend their self-concept. And it remains a consistent aspect throughout different stages of life. This is the most crucial part of a person's development, and it represents the foundation of who they will become in the future. The failure of not tapping into my identity caused a lot of confusion and uncertainty, which led me to experience mental illness. I began seeking validation through my relationships and so-called friendships, which spiraled out of control.

I started attending Sam Houston State University located near Houston, Texas, in 2003 after leaving a local community college in Fort Worth, where my parents wanted me to attend. I had a deep, strong desire to leave my parents' home and to escape my structured upbringing, and I no longer wanted to live by my parents' rules anymore. Realistically I was not ready for the level of exposure and freedom that was associated with college life, but I was grown, and no one was going to hold me back.

Due to my childhood trauma, I was often led by my emotions, resulting in making poor decisions as I navigated life. I continued to mask the pain and turned to pleasures that temporarily satisfied my flesh like drugs, sex, and alcohol, thinking it would finally fill the void. My goal was to mask the pain, a very common strategy that many people resort to when trying to help themselves cope with physical and emotional stress. Ultimately through my actions, it created more trauma bonds, and I found myself trapped in toxic soul-ties that resulted in increased depression and anxiety. Continuing to pile hurt on top of hurt later resulted in a catastrophic disaster. The six-year-old little girl inside of me was desperately crying out for help, but no one was able to hear her because of the mask I continued to wear.

Have you ever been in a season where you didn't know if you are coming or going? It's like everything that can go wrong is going wrong. This is why I can relate to how you currently feel or have felt at some point in your life. Silently crying out for help and no one hears you—but rest assure that God hears our every cry.

The Bible says in **Psalm 34:17**: *The righteous cry out, and the Lord hears them; he delivers them from all their troubles.*

This scripture tells us that no matter what you are facing, God cares for you, He hears you, and He's all that you need. I had countless people who I called "friends" in my life, and I even joined a sorority my sophomore year at Sam Houston State, but no matter the amount of people I was surrounded by, deep down I was still crying out for help. I was on a path of self-destruction, but I didn't quite know how to break myself free.

As my life continued to spiral out of control, I became very defensive with my family and other loved ones who genuinely cared about me, but I couldn't see their efforts because I was blinded by the pain. The pain that I thought I was good at masking started to become my identity through rage, anger, bitterness, and regrets. I didn't even realize it. Self-sabotaging behavior became my norm. I used self-sabotaging as my coping mechanism to deal with stressful situations and the rejection. It made my problems even worse by limiting my ability to successfully move forward in a healthy way. I felt like I was letting everyone down—my family, my true friends, and most importantly myself.

It was April the year of 2004 after returning to Sam Houston from visiting my parents for Easter break, and on top of everything that I was dealing with, I found out that I was pregnant. I was so devastated, and it felt like my life was completely over. I was only nineteen years old; there was absolutely no way that I could add another title and a new level of pressure into my life, especially being someone's mother with all the issues I had. Seriously, God? At that point, I knew that God had checked out of my life a long time ago, just like everyone else had previously done, and now I was left to pick up the pieces by myself. So many thoughts ran through my mind, and many were not good. I just wanted to escape the pressures of my poor decisions, but I couldn't. I had to face the consequences of my actions. I was forced to grow up and take responsibility for my own life. The choice was mine to make if I wanted to experience change.

My parents were disappointed but never stopped loving me; they continued to show me through their actions. Deep down I knew that God loved me, too, because what I deemed to be a hinderance in my life, getting pregnant, was the best thing that had ever happened to me. Of course I didn't realize it at the beginning because life became hard—real fast. After finishing up my spring semester, I decided to move back home permanently until I had my baby boy. I wasn't too thrilled about moving back home, under my parents' strict rules, but at that point, I had no choice. When we are desperate for change to take place, it often requires us to get uncomfortable.

As my life reached a pivotal point while sitting inside my parents' home, it allowed me the time to do a lot of self-reflection. I began to ask myself what I wanted out of life. What kind of mother did I want to be for my son? How did I get here? I wanted to experience change, but what did that really mean or look like? What kind of life did God want me to have? What was my purpose in life? Have you ever been in this position or in such state of mind before? If so, please know that what you are currently feeling is okay. We have all been here at some point in our lives, but what happens next is what really matters. Are you going to continue down the path of destruction or turn away from all your wicked ways, asking God to extend His forgiveness over your life and reclaim your faith in Christ? Well, that is exactly the route I decided to take; I made a choice. No matter how far I went astray, I always knew the way back home in Christ our heavenly Father. God loves us so much; He sent His only son to be born, wrapped in flesh to bear all our sins on the cross. That is the truest definition and example of pure love.

The Bible says in ***John 3:16****: For God so loved the world that he gave his one and only Son, that whoever believes in him shall not perish but have eternal life.*

Romans 8:1*: There is therefore now no condemnation to those who are in Christ Jesus, who do not walk according to the flesh, but according to the Spirit.*

This scripture tells us that we serve a God of a second chance. No matter if you are a believer or non-believer, God's love is eternal; His forgiveness and salvation is available to all, because He paid the price on the cross when Jesus died for you and me.

CHAPTER 3: SETTLING FOR LESS

God desires the very best for His children, but often we stand in the way of receiving His blessings and become our own hindrance. My season of settling for less represents me operating out of my own flesh and will. Can you relate? The desire of the flesh is set against the desires of the Spirit. Let's break this down a little more.

The Bible says in **Galatians 5:19–21**: *Now the works of the flesh are evident, which are: adultery, fornication, uncleanness, lewdness, idolatry, sorcery, hatred, contentions, jealousies, outbursts of wrath, selfish ambitions, dissensions, heresies, envy, murders, drunkenness, revelries, and the like; of which I tell you beforehand, just as I also told you in time past, that those who practice such things will not inherit the kingdom of God.*

This scripture tells us that when we operate out of the flesh, we can easily be manipulated and used by the enemy. As I continued to navigate the unwavering waters of life while trying to pick up the broken pieces on my own, I was still battling a war from within. After I gave birth to my son in 2004, I knew that I needed to get my life together to provide for him and to be someone who he would be proud to call Mom one day. Still wearing the weights of disappointment from my parents and others, I began down a road of overachieving, believing that I could make my wrongs right. I thought that if I worked extremely hard to finish college, landed a good job, made lots of money, became successful, and finally got married, maybe then everyone would be happy for me and overlook all the poor decisions I had previously made. Boy! Was I so wrong.

I was blessed to finish college, and I graduated with a bachelor of science in health administration in 2012, and I obtained my master of business administration in 2014. I started working in auto collections and quickly moved to the banking and finance industry, climbing the corporate ladder. I was blessed to work for some of the top major banks worldwide and later obtained my real estate license in 2016. I purchased my first home as a single woman and achieved the American dream by owning real estate, but something was still missing from within. I was so focused on proving a point and desiring to feel accepted I began to lose myself once again.

Although my parents were so proud of my achievements and the goals I had set forth for myself, there was still a void. I even settled for two marriages that were not ordained by God, which ultimately ended in two divorces, resulting in more loss, disappointment, and rejection. I was still searching deeply for something that would eliminate my pain that I had carried for many years. I settled for an autopilot version of myself, while repeating the same cycles over and over again. Jonathan McReynolds has a song called "Cycles," and my life journey has been a true depiction. It talks about how the enemy will try to keep us bound in repeating the same cycles, never being able to break completely free. When true healing has not been manifested in your life, past hurts that are suppressed always tends to resurface when one is provoked or triggered. Like a continuing sequel. The devil knows you more than you know yourself because he learns from our mistakes, and he always tempts us with things that displease and separate us from God.

The Bible says in ***John 10:10***: *The thief does not come except to steal, and to kill, and to destroy. I have come that they may have life, and that they may have it more abundantly.*

This scripture tells us that the devil has only one assignment, and he will do anything and everything to accomplish his goal. However, there is no need to fear, because there is power in the name of Jesus, and when we speak His name out loud, the devil must flee. But the choice is yours if you allow him to come back in by repeating those same old, tired cycles. The stronghold must be broken.

The Bible says in ***Genesis 50:20***: *But as for you, you meant evil against me; but God meant it for good, in order to bring it about as it is this day, to save many people alive.*

My season of settling for less also reminds me of the children of Israel and how they were forced to spend forty years in the wilderness before finally entering the Promised Land. Ultimately, this was a punishment from God for their disobedience and lack of faith. During their journey traveling back and forth across the desert, they traveled on the same old roads time and time again but never reached their destination. How frustrating can that be? They even faced many challenges, but God still showed them favor and provision by showering down miracles.

The part that really stood out to me in this powerful Bible story was that their journey to the Promised Land should have only taken eleven days. When we are operating outside of the will of God, He will withhold blessings from us until we are ready. If God had allowed the Israelites to enter the Promised Land prematurely, they would have probably destroyed themselves, and matters would have gotten even worse. I am so glad that we serve a God who can see our beginning and our ending; He knows what is best for us and in His timing. Even though the Israelites faced a great deal of adversity, they never gave up, despite the struggles, doubts, rejection, and fears. They finally overcame their test and received the ultimate triumph. God gave the Israelites beauty for their ashes, and He beautifully rebuilt their lives again.

We serve an amazing God, and His word says in Psalm 37 to delight yourself also in the Lord, and He shall give you the desires of your heart. This scripture tells us not to settle for a mediocre life and, most importantly, not to settle for less. He desires more for you, and so do I.

The Bible says in **Isaiah 40:31**: *But those who wait upon the Lord shall renew their strength; they shall mount up with wings as eagles; they shall run, and not be weary; and they shall walk, and not faint.*

James 4:6, 10: *But He gives more grace. Therefore He says, "God resists the proud, but gives grace to the humble. Humble yourselves in the sight of the Lord, and He will lift you up.*

Oftentimes waiting is a part of the process when God is rebuilding you. Waiting on God involves trusting Him patiently; we may not understand the "why," but trust me, it is worth the wait. Humility and strength are built by waiting and putting your faith in God. There is no doubt about it; developing humility is tough, but God commands it. Before settling for a lesser version of you, remember that we cannot be who God wants us to be without a waiting season. It's through our waiting that we learn to stand strong in God and grow our faith in Him alone.

CHAPTER 4: THE BREAKING

Many people in this world are living their lives trying to maintain a false perception of "perfection," and we should not pressure ourselves trying to achieve something that is only perceived as an illusion. Let's dive into this a little more; people on Instagram and Facebook only post what they want you to see: the good parts in their lives, the flawless pictures, the dream vacations, the achievements, and the happiest of moments. But if you allow yourself to get caught up in only the good times in life and never focus on what really matters, you will literally drive yourself crazy. If men and women would dare to be bold enough by living fearlessly, everything we see on social media would look completely different. There is a level of freedom that is indescribable when you decide to live a fearless life and not care about the opinions of others.

I personally made a conscious decision to walk in boldness and be transparent about how broken I was for so long. I completely understand why that part of your story isn't so attractive and might not get as many "likes" on Instagram or Facebook. It's something about being real with yourself and with God that begins to open the door to authenticity. The real beauty is that God protected you from it all, and it is allowing God to bring healing in the areas we normally don't post about on social media. He uses every broken piece of you and helps to put you back together again; it's all a part of the rebuilding process. It may look ugly at first, but God always gives us beauty for our ashes. It's one thing to be broken from life's pain and disappointments, but if you take a moment to reflect over your life, you would have to agree that you were beautifully broken, and God did not allow the devil to have the victory. To be used by God to build up His kingdom, there are things that must be broken off and removed out of our lives before His will can be manifested.

We are all perfect in God's eyes, just the way we arc; He created us. God tell us in His word to love our neighbors as ourselves. For me, it was extremely difficult to even love myself, while constantly feeling the pressure of living a life of perfection. Being a preacher's kid doesn't mean that you are closer to God than anyone else. It seemed like I was targeted by the devil even more. Our faith is not guaranteed because of our parents' roles or positions within the church. I personally have questioned my own faith on several occasions, and I've had many moments of uncertainty. But I am grateful for my parents modeling the Christian lifestyle for my sister and I while growing up, but when I became an adult, knowing right from wrong, I had to accept Christ as Lord and Savior over my life for myself.

The Bible says in **Romans 10:13**: *For whosoever calls on the name of the Lord shall be saved.*

As we continue to discover the beauty in the rebuilding, I will reveal more on how and when I truly accepted God as Lord over my life, which led me to experience God for myself. I'm sure you are thinking, "Didn't she already accept Christ into her life before?" And the answer is "yes." Well, I didn't always get it right and had to pray on many occasions,

"Lord, if you get me out of this one, I will never do this again!" And I ended up repeating the same old mistakes again and again. Now that I am an adult, I choose to live a surrendered life. My parents were not perfect and made many mistakes, like all parents, including myself. Not everyone is fortunate to have both parents who were actively present in their lives while growing up. They loved me and wanted to help ensure my sister and I achieved happiness, success, and most importantly, knowing God who is our rock and foundation.

My "breaking" season was when my entire life started to change. In this season I had reached the lowest and darkest point in my life's journey. I was so tired, and I didn't have any more fight in me to live within the parameters of my own will. I disconnected myself from the people I loved the most and individuals who I thought would fill my empty void. Sadly, I got to the point where I no longer wanted to live. Even though I was extremely successful and accomplished in everything I had set forth for myself, I literally didn't want anything besides freedom from "ME."

First I started to self-isolate from my community; I fell prey to the enemy, and he started to speak to me again, just as he did with Eve in the Garden of Eden before the fall of man. His voice was subtle yet chilling, conniving, and calculated as he started to whisper lies into my heart…"No one loves you; no one will ever understand you; don't continue to live with the rejection and pain…death is the easiest way out." I thought to myself, maybe it is my only option to finally escape the constant nightmare I've been living for many years. This was my way out, and my mind was made up, not even caring that I had an amazing son to raise. I knew that he would be taken care of by his father and my family. My desperation for freedom of the mind overpowered everyone and everything I truly loved.

One night I went out with so-called friends—while still hiding behind a mask and saying to myself that I was "okay"—and decided to get extremely wasted. I became very reckless, and that is when I made a conscious decision to drive home, and no one intervened. It was around three o'clock in the morning; I was on Highway 121 and had just passed the MacArthur exit in Lewisville, driving in the middle lane, no other cars around. That is when I literally fell asleep behind the wheel, while traveling eighty-five-plus mph. I was only two exits away from where I lived, but making it home was not a concern for me; I wanted to finally be free. On that very morning, I heard the voice of the Holy Spirit for the first time in my entire life. I knew it was His voice because it immediately brought forth so much peace and calmness into my spirit. "Jessica, Jessica!" the voice spoke so vividly. As soon as I heard my name, I jumped up just in time to turn my steering wheel to the right to avoid hitting the guardrail, which would have resulted in my car falling from an eighty- to one-hundred-foot-tall bridge.

The Bible says in ***John 10:27***: *My sheep hear my voice, and I know them, and they follow me.*

God spared my life, and I am a living witness! From that moment on, I knew that my life would never be the same. Something changed in me, and I immediately started to feel different. When I finally made it home, I fell to my knees, crying out to God. He showed me mercy. All these years of me hearing testimonies from other people of how God performed miracles in their lives, and I could finally relate. No longer would I settle for living my life on autopilot, going around and around as if I was on a hamster wheel. This time I desperately wanted God to change my life, and finally I was ready to surrender to His will. I knew that I was nothing without God.

I began living my life intentionally. I developed a prayer life, reading His word, and attending church more frequently, while seeking after God. The moment I heard His voice, peace showered down over me, and I needed to experience His touch again. I became desperate.

The Bible says in ***Psalm 42:1****: As the deer pants for the water brooks, so pants my soul for You, O God.*

When you are in the presence of God, nothing else in this world matters. I humbled myself and truly allowed God into my heart, as He began putting my broken pieces back together. While devoting uninterrupted time to study His word, God began to reveal the purpose behind my pain.

The Bible says in ***Isaiah 54:17****: No weapon formed against me shall proper, and every tongue which rises against you in judgement, You shall condemn.*

Luke 10:19*: Behold, I give you the authority to trample on serpents and scorpions, and over all the power of the enemy, and nothing shall by any means hurt you.*

In these scriptures God was showing me that despite the enemy's plans he had plotted against me, God's hand of protection remained over my life even before I was formed in my mother's womb and when I suddenly stopped breathing when I was just a few weeks old. His word didn't say that the weapons were not going to be formed but instead that none of them would prosper. So I asked God, "What was the purpose behind my pain?" As I closed my eyes, He started giving me a vision. I began to see a beautiful blue sky and not a cloud in sight, as if I were looking at a blank canvas. Then, suddenly, God started writing out the letters **P.A.I.N.** but in a vertical order in shiny, pure white clouds. Mind you, this was not a dream I had; it was a vision that was released directly from heaven. And I was wide awake and eager to know why the devil had been fighting me for so many years as if I had a big red target on my back and why my journey looked so different from others'. God then started to fill in the meaning of each letter.

P: Planned
A: Attacks
I: Increase
N: Newness

Once I was able to clearly see and understand what God was speaking to me, it all started to make sense. All the years that I had questioned if God was with me in pain, in the abuse, in the rejection, in the failed marriages, and in the suicide attempt. I knew then that God was right there by my side every step of the way, and no matter what I did, His grace never fell short. Newness was God's ultimate plan for my life, which refers to the state or quality of being new. Elevation often comes through vehicles of tests and trials after separation has taken place. God was doing a new thing in my life, but it required me to first die to my old self. God didn't give up on me, and neither will He give up on you.

The Bible says in **Psalm 51:10**: *Create in me a clean heart, O God, and renew a steadfast spirit within in me.*

Isaiah 43:19*: Behold, I will do a new thing, now it shall spring forth; shall you not know it?*

I will even make a road in the wilderness, and rivers in the desert.

These scriptures describe the beginning of God revealing the beauty in my rebuilding process, cleaning out the old version of me and restoring my entire life. God gave me a blank canvas, but this time He was guiding me as if I was the paintbrush and He the painter, giving me beauty for my ashes that started to become a beautiful masterpiece. Deep down inside I knew that God was preparing to use my life as a testimony, and it was crucial that I expressed willingness to accept His call.

CHAPTER 5: THE STAGES OF HEALING

Now it is time for me to challenge you once again. Ask yourself: what needs to be healed, restored, and renewed in your life? And don't forget to write it down in a journal or create a vision board of things or behaviors that you desire for God to touch and heal. Writing it down will help you to stay accountable. Change is not always easily accepted, and many individuals struggle with it. I define change as kryptonite to a comfort zone; it's inevitable to experience external change without first embracing the internal change that begins from within. What is internal will begin to reflect outwardly at some point. If your insides are toxic, filled with drama, lies, and deceit, those behaviors will become your identity. It is crucial to develop a relationship with God during your "breaking" season and allow Him to become your strong foundation.

Here are some ways to help you develop a relationship with God:

- Study God's word.
- Act on the word. (Faith without works is dead).
- Listen and pray to God.
- Look to the Holy Spirit to comfort you, praying for His peace and guidance.
- Follow God's commandments and will for your life.
- Live a surrendered life, start a gratitude journal.
- Worship God.

It is impossible for God to begin rebuilding your life without first addressing step number one. Who do you serve? Are you a true believer in Christ? Have you confessed your sins to Him and accepted Christ into your heart? I welcomed Christ into my life at very young age; I knew God through the teachings I heard growing up in church, but it wasn't until I was an adult that I experienced God for myself. It's about having a real relationship versus just knowing the religion. When I was in the depths of my pain, God met me there. When I wanted to give up on life and I no longer had a desire to live, God met me there. When so-called friends turned their backs on me, God met me there. When I was hopeless and didn't have peace of mind, God met me there. And God continues to meet me where I am. He is the way, the truth, and the life found in John 14:6.

The Bible says in **Psalm 46:1**: *God is our refuge and strength, an ever-present help in trouble.*

This scripture tells us that no matter the mistakes we've made, the many disappointments we've experienced, the rejection, the setbacks, and the heartbreaks, God still loves us. He wants to help you, and the only thing in the moment you must do is surrender your life to Him. Cry if you need to; crying is healthy for the soul, and it's okay. Surrender all the heavy burdens that are weighing you down. God did not create us to bear the weight and pressure of our own lives but instead to cast all our anxiety on him because He cares for us, which is found in 1 Peter 5:7.

May I pray for you?
Dear Heavenly Father,

First I want to give you thanks for allowing us to see another beautiful day. Right now, Lord, I pray for my brother and my sister who are reading this. I ask that you meet them in the midst of their brokenness, the hurt, the pain, and their fears. You know exactly what they are facing in this moment, so dear Lord, I speak healing, restoration, deliverance, newness, and chains being broken off their lives right now. I ask that you remove pride, people, things, and behaviors that no longer serve their purpose and ask you to release the blessings that have been held up in heaven due to their disobedience. Save, heal, and restore their lives as you begin to reveal the beauty in their rebuilding, Amen.

Now I want you to repeat after me…
Dear Lord,

I am a sinner and please have mercy on me, O God. Wash away all my iniquity and cleanse me from my sins. I welcome you into my heart, God, and I want to be changed from the inside out. God, I believe that you gave us your son Jesus as a sacrifice, and He died on the cross for my sins and rose on the third day. God, I ask that you start rebuilding my life today. Thank you for your grace and your mercy in Jesus's name, Amen.

Congratulations!!! You have taken the first step in your rebuilding process.

You may be wondering why change is a requirement in the healing process: it's simple! When you make a conscious decision to openly embrace change in your life, it eliminates the fears that come with change. Fully embracing change pushes you outside of your comfort zone, and that is when courage begins to grow. Comfort zones can be dangerous places to settle in, and they also hinder you from experiencing the life God intended for you to have.

Have you ever felt like you had to get your own life together before presenting yourself to God? This is a lie from the pits of hell; God desires you just as you are, every broken and shattered piece. He will clean you up, starting from the inside out. Many people have asked me, "When did God change your life for the better? How did He do it? What did the process look like?" First I made a conscious decision to seek out professional counseling, because I knew that I was not equipped to do it on my own. I was intentional about doing the work this time, but I needed someone to help keep me accountable as I embarked upon uncharted territory.

The Bible says in ***James 2:26****: For as the body without the spirit is dead, so faith without works is dead also.*

That is when God brought Honour Sitholé, MA, LPC-S, owner and founder of Inside Fitness, into my life to help guide me on the road to healing. What I liked most about working with Honour as my counselor, he is a believer in Christ, providing me with a biblical aspect of my life's journey as we often navigated back into my past, addressing the roots of my pain. He strongly believed that unresolved emotional pain makes it difficult to obtain and maintain a clear perspective on life. He created a judgment-free zone, which allowed me to finally be transparent and vulnerable about things I was too afraid to talk about. For me to experience true healing from my past, I had to literally face and address my demons head on. I had lied to myself for so many years that I had suppressed the pain, but I was wrong. The hurtful emotions were always there but laid dormant until triggered, and addressing them was the only way to get through them and overcome.

I wrote my letters to the individuals and situations that brought me the most pain and poured out all the emotions that were bottled up deep inside. There were days that I cried my eyelashes off, and times when I wanted to give up, but I didn't. Not only did I have to forgive myself, but I had to forgive the individuals that hurt me. Forgiveness brings us closer to the Lord, releases us from bitterness, and deepens our relationship with God. God's strength was made perfect in my weakness (2 Corinthians 12:9), and I was solely dependent on Him as I was guided by Honour, my counselor. God instructed me to see my problems as a ladder, enabling me to climb up and to see my life from His perspective. Once my perspective was heightened, I was equipped to look away from focusing my attention solely onto the problems, while turning my full attention to God. The light of His presence was shining down upon me. Honour was a vessel who God used to help rebuild my life, and I am extremely grateful that our life paths crossed. He kept me accountable to do the work, desired more for my life, and applied God's word as a light onto my path as I dared to never live my life outside of the parameters of God's will.

As you embark upon your own personal healing journey, more than likely it will look different from mine. Many people may not agree with me seeing a counselor, and it may be frowned upon, but it was a part of the blueprint that God intended for me to experience.

The Bible says in **Proverbs 27:17**: *As iron sharpens iron, so a man sharpens the countenance of his friend.*

My prayer is that you seek God for direction on how to start your healing journey. Here are six steps to my healing journey, and I hope that you find this information helpful. However, your path maybe more or less, but I challenge you to apply these steps into your own life and know that, if taken seriously, your life will begin to change for the better. Trust me! I am living proof.

The Beauty in Rebuilding
6 Steps to my Healing Journey…

1. Welcome God into your heart; ask Him for forgiveness for living outside of His will.
2. Understand that healing takes time and it's a process. It is important to exercise patience in this season by giving yourself grace. Healing is not a sprint.
3. Don't settle for the "fillers." Fillers are temporary, and whatever is temporary will NEVER be enough (people, places, and things that only serve the flesh and not your spirit).
4. Be willing to live a surrendered life. Develop a relationship with God; spend time in His word while removing all distractions. Daily devotions really helped me. —*Jesus Calling* by Sarah Young.
5. Get involved in a ministry within your church; if you don't have a church home, seek God's direction for the right church. Get Planted! Being in community with the right people will help you stay accountable to do the work.
6. Seek professional counseling. Pray that God will align you with the right person to help you. Know that you cannot do it alone, and dare to live outside of your comfort zones. There is strength in asking for help!

CHAPTER 6:
THE EVOLUTION OF YOU

My life's journey has reflected the metamorphosis process of a butterfly. Butterflies are a symbol of transformation and change. Each stage of the transformation process birthed a new level in my life, signifying both inner and outer growth and an opportunity to learn something new about myself in each stage. As stated by butterflyidentification.com, butterflies hold a profound cultural significance in many societies around the world, not only symbolizing transformation but also a rebirth and the soul's journey. Every stage in my life consists of ups and downs, uncertainties, fears, rejection, and disappointments. But throughout every stage it also introduced a new level of dependence on God and vulnerability to trust God through the process. I had to walk by faith knowing that God was always in control. God is in control of everything—every process, every dark moment, and every breakthrough that leads to rebuilding. When the metamorphosis cycle of a butterfly is complete, it brings forth a new life, a new look, a new shape, and new abilities. And most importantly a new mindset.

The Bible says in ***2 Corinthians 5:17****: Therefore, if anyone is in Christ, he is a new creation; old things have passed away; behold, all things have become new.*

This scripture describes how a butterfly now has the capability of flying to NEW heights, never to settle for crawling around in the low places ever again unless it chooses to. Remember, the choice is yours! Repeating the same old cycles and expecting different results is the definition of lunacy. Your appetite for change must be greater than your will to remain the same. You must be willing to experience real change by leveling up your palate as God brings you to a place of elevation. God desires to have a relationship with us. He wants us to choose Him, talk to Him, spend time reading His word, just like He chose us and sent Jesus to die for our sins on the cross.

Let's break this down a little more. There are four stages of a butterfly's life cycle, and each stage looks different and serves its own purpose. During my healing journey, I was able to clearly see how the development of a caterpillar into a beautiful butterfly mirrored the seasons of my life. The *Webster's Dictionary* describes how a butterfly experiences a series of changes in shape, form, and activities that it goes through during its lifetime in the life cycle. When God begins to rebuild your life from the inside out, He performs a metamorphosis process by removing the old and introducing the new, refined you. Certain relationships, people, and things are removed out of your DNA, and God replaces them with His will, a new heart and mindset.

Stage 1: The Egg (The Mother's Womb)

The egg stage is described as "the mother's womb." It's the place where you are sustained by the protection of the Creator. You are in your purest of forms, with no fears, no shame, no disappointments, rejection, or pain. Life is good without a care in the world because there is covering and overflowing love.

The Bible says in ***Jeremiah 1:5****: "Before I formed you in the womb I knew you; before you were born I sanctified you; I ordained you a prophet to the nations.*

This scripture should give you some comfort, knowing that God knows and loves you. He created your blueprint and knew everything that would take place in your life. He is the potter, and we are the clay to be molded and refined by God. His plans toward you are of good and not of evil, as it says in Jeremiah 29:11. Many are the plans of a person's heart, but it is the Lord's purpose that prevails, which is found in Proverbs 19:21.

Stage 2: The Caterpillar (Life Choices)

The caterpillar stage describes the choices I made in my life resulting from the unhealed trauma that occurred. I'm most certain that the caterpillar cannot fully grasp its full growth potential while in its current form. Just as I settled for less in my life, allowing the fillers of the world to distract me as I tried my best to mask the pain. Fillers are known as distractions. When our minds are so clouded with the things of this world, we tend to lose sight of who we are, blinded by the enemy's schemes. As I tried to navigate life while settling for an autopilot version of myself, I became numb to the deeply rooted pain that ultimately became my identity. When we are in the midst of our pain, the devil starts to introduce "fillers" into our lives. Distractions are defined as the act of distracting, a drawing apart or separation.

The Bible says in **Isaiah 59:2**: *But your iniquities have separated you from your God; your sins have hidden his face from you, so that he will not hear.*

This scripture tells us that when we fall short of God's glory by allowing our flesh to take the lead, it separates us from God, and He is displeased. The devil rejoices when we fall because he knows it is another step toward destroying the plans of God over our lives.

Here are some examples of dangerous fillers that the devils try to distract us with:

- Social media
- Excessive spending
- Staying too busy, excessive planning, and work schedules
- Self-aggrandizement

- The need to over accomplish
- Adultery/Fornication
- Drugs or consuming excessive alcohol

My major filler was when I settled into two marriages, believing that it was God's will for my life. I thought that my spouse would ultimately help to mend my deeply rooted brokenness, but I was so wrong. I found myself even more broken than I originally was going into the marriage. Although I experienced two divorces, I believe that God places certain people in our lives to teach us things about ourselves, and they both taught me that I failed at loving myself. Self-love was something that I lacked for so many years, and it forced me to start working on myself, not knowing that my life would never be the same again. When I finally embraced self-love, I made a vow that I would never settle for the broken version of me ever again. Self-love is our responsibility and should be a nonnegotiable. My caterpillar season prepared me to begin opening my heart to receive the life God always intended for me to have.

Stage 3: The Pupa (My Transformation)

The pupa stage describes the darkest season of my life when I no longer had the desire to live. It was the time when I came to know God for myself; He rescued me from "me" the night I tried to end my life. God met me in my pain and started to give me the peace that I was searching for all my life. Just like the butterfly as it enters the pupa stage—during this process it is hidden by leaves or buried underground. It is exactly how I describe this season, as I felt trapped in my dark place. I was filled with anxiety and depression, unable to break my mind free. There was nothing that I could do to get myself out of my own cocoon of darkness, but God turned my darkest place and used it for His glory. Just like the butterfly, the cocoon stage plays a major part of its process and is deemed necessary before elevation can be manifested.

My life had reached an all-time low, and there was no way to go but up at that point. I just didn't know how to accomplish such a task, exhausting all my options I had initially tried. After rededicating my life to Christ, God kept on reminding me that His strength would be made perfect in my weakness, but I had to start depending on Him. I believe that God created my own metamorphosis process, and it was up to me to activate my trust in Him, even in the darkest times in my life. God is in control of every season we go through, but we must trust His will. In my transformation stage, God started to prune the things in my life that no longer served my purpose. Certain people, old cycles, and pride were removed out of my life, and it honestly felt good. It felt as if heavy burdens had been released from my life.

The Bible says in **Hebrews 12:1**: *Therefore we also, since we are surrounded by so great a cloud of witnesses, let us lay aside every weight, and the sin which so easily ensnares us, and let us run with endurance the race that is set before us.*

Matthew 11:28–30: *Come to me, all you who are weary and burdened, and I will give you rest. Take my yoke upon you and learn from me, for I am gentle and humble in heart, and you will find rest for your souls. For my yoke is easy and my burden is light.*

These scriptures tell us that we must be willing to let go of the things that hinder us from experiencing real change and elevation in our lives. I challenge you to allow God to prune you to prepare you for what will be. He has a plan and purpose for your life. Transformation is not a one-time event; it's a continual journey of becoming the best version of you. As of today I am still learning new things about myself, and it feels amazing. Getting to know the real Jessica at my core has been the most freeing feeling I have ever had, and I'm no longer weighed down by the trauma. Yes! You and I will continue to make mistakes; remember that we are still human and give yourself grace in the moments you fall short. Remember that there is no condemnation for those who belong to God found in Romans 8:1. Every day is a new day to allow God's word to transform your mindset and bring forth newness, because true change first begins internally, starting with your mind. He can see all your flaws and failures and still love you with unfailing love.

***Romans 12:2–3**: And be not conformed to this world: but be transformed by the renewing of your mind, that ye may prove what is that good, and acceptable, and perfect, will of God.*

Stage 4: The Butterfly (My Exodus)

The butterfly stage described my exodus season. Breaking free from the dark place of the cocoon indicated that God was blessing me with a new life. I was finally ready for God to elevate me. God broke me free from what once held me bound; the environment that protected me in one season no longer served a purpose in my life, and it had to release me. Just like Jonah in the Bible when the whale swallowed him for a season. But when it was time for Jonah to fulfill his assignment, God made the whale release him. If the butterfly remained in its egg or pupa stage, its growth potential would become detrimental to its life cycle. This is a prime example of why the pruning season is so important. When you fully surrender to God's will, allowing Him to prune you, it is a crucial part of the rebuilding process. Old mindsets can't hold new blessings.

The Bible says in **Matthew 9:17**: *Nor do they put new wine into old wineskins, or else the wineskins break, the wine is spilled, and the wineskins are ruined. But they put new wine into new wineskins, and both are preserved.*

During this season I was able to view my pain from the lens of God's perspective, realizing that it was exactly what needed to take place. My counselor mentioned to me during one of our sessions that, "We have to clean out all of the bad stuff before the wounds can begin to heal." I finally had reached the point in my healing journey to fully understand the magnitude of why God allowed certain things to take place in my life. My mind was renewed, and God continued to restore my brokenness. No longer would I seek validation from people, places, or things. In that moment I knew exactly who and whose I was, and no devil in hell was going to stop me anymore. Even when I tried to take the life God gave to me when He formed me in my mother's womb, He still protected me. God restored my soul, and I am forever grateful God filled the hole in my heart and the deeply rooted pain and trauma. God delivered me from ME, and the devil was forced to release his hands off my life. I am covered by the blood of Jesus.

The cocoon also represented death to my old self, and a new life was on the verge of being birthed into my purpose. When transition takes place, it means that something must die. It's similar to when God finally calls you home, and you take your last breath.

The Bible says in **2 Corinthians 5:8**: *We are confident, yes, well pleased rather to be absent from the body and to be present with the Lord.*

Whether it is an old version of yourself, a mindset, behaviors, or cycles that don't serve a purpose, they must die before the new you can be resurrected. YOU play a manager role within your rebuilding process. To fully embrace the evolution of you, you must be willing to **Y**ield, **O**vercome, and be **U**nstoppable.

- **Y: Yield to God's will.**
- **O: Overcome the things that no longer serve a purpose in your life.**
- **U: Be Unstoppable by displaying resilience and determination to do the work to experience true healing.**

A butterfly is proof that you can go through a great deal of darkness yet become something beautiful, but you must trust the process.

CHAPTER 7: CONCLUSION

We have covered so much, and I hope that you have been encouraged and ultimately blessed. My prayer is that I have given you the necessary tools to begin your journey on the road to discovering the beauty in your rebuilding. In this book I revealed how I overcame being a victim of child molestation, dealt with the pressures of being a preacher's kid, became a mom at a young age, attempted suicide, and allowed God to rebuild my life after experiencing two failed marriages. This book was birthed out of my pain and I am a true testament that God's love and mercy never fails. I am determined to live on purpose and be obedient to whatever God instructs me to do; I am a willing vessel.

There will be many times when you feel as if it is impossible to truly trust God on your path to healing and overcoming past trauma. Trust me! The process was not easy, but it is possible with God. I believe this is why God planted the desire in me to write this book, as a living and breathing testimony that there is life after pain. Do not continue to allow your past to be your identity or dictate the future you settle for; desire more for your own life. Dare to heal, starting from the inside out. Be willing to do the work and the challenges that I have set forth for you in this book, remembering that, often it gets messy before are you able to see the beauty that lies deeply within. You may be in your caterpillar stage of the process, but know that there is so much peace and beauty on the other side of your healing journey. No matter the mistakes you've made, God's grace is sufficient, and His love is everlasting.

The Bible says in ***2 Corinthians 12:9***: *And He said to me, "My grace is sufficient for you, for My strength is made perfect in weakness." Therefore, most gladly I will rather boast in my infirmities, that the power of Christ may rest upon me.*

This scripture reveals that, when I am at my weakest, I am strong in Christ. God is fully aware of your situation, and He will not allow you to be tempted beyond what you are able to bear, as it says in 1 Corinthians 10:13. The darkness that once had a stronghold over my life started to give way to the light as I began to open up about my past. Although my past does not define me or my future, it is a part of my life's journey and now my God-given testimony. Are you ready to unlock a new version of yourself? When you are beautifully broken by God, discovering the true beauty in your rebuilding process becomes easy. Let God restore your life. God loves you and so do I.

Be blessed!

RESOURCES

I have navigated the effects of mental illness, and taking care of your mental health is extremely important to me. I take mental health awareness very seriously, and I am an advocate to help people that are hopeless to find hope again. If you are struggling with thoughts of suicide, please know that you are not alone and your life matters to me, and most importantly to God. There is help and resources available to you, and I strongly encourage you to make the call.

988 Suicide and Crisis Lifeline
Languages: English, Spanish
Hours: Available 24 hours

Today is a great day to be alive.

REFERENCES

Merriam-Webster: America's Most Trusted Dictionary. www.merriam-webster.com

Sasha. 2023. *What Do Butterflies Symbolize? The Complete Guide to the Spiritual Meaning of Butterflies.* http://vitalethos.com.

Milton Keynes UK
Ingram Content Group UK Ltd.
UKHW022227251124
451566UK00007B/154